# The Book of
# DINOSAURS

## A COMPLETE ILLUSTRATED HISTORY

## DERRYDALE BOOKS
### New York • Avenel

# Contents

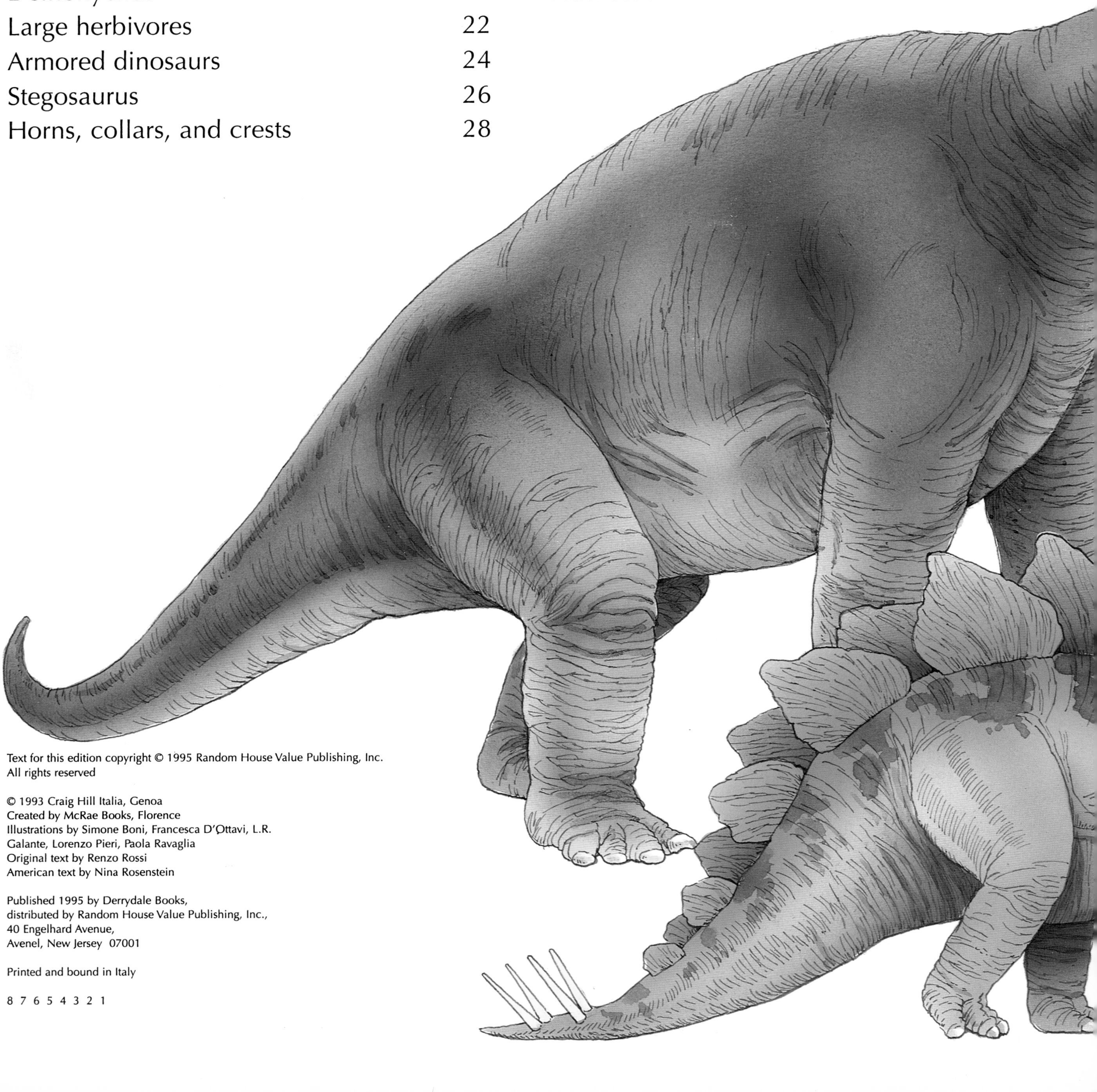

Text for this edition copyright © 1995 Random House Value Publishing, Inc.
All rights reserved

© 1993 Craig Hill Italia, Genoa
Created by McRae Books, Florence
Illustrations by Simone Boni, Francesca D'Ottavi, L.R.
Galante, Lorenzo Pieri, Paola Ravaglia
Original text by Renzo Rossi
American text by Nina Rosenstein

Published 1995 by Derrydale Books,
distributed by Random House Value Publishing, Inc.,
40 Engelhard Avenue,
Avenel, New Jersey 07001

Printed and bound in Italy

8 7 6 5 4 3 2 1

*Brachiosaurus*

*Tyrannosaurus*

*Stegosaurus*

# Dinosaurs today

Picture the world millions of years ago. A dinosaur may have stood right in the spot where you are now! Of course, the earth looked very different back then. When the first dinosaurs lived, much of the earth was a desert. Then, slowly, the weather changed. Forests grew; swamps and shallow oceans spread across the land. This took millions of years. Many, many different kinds of dinosaurs lived and died during this time.

No human being has ever met a dinosaur, but we know that they existed because people have discovered their bones. When the first huge dinosaur bones were found by accident in England almost two hundred years ago, no one knew what they were. Were they from a giant elephant, or some sort of strange monster? Since then, paleontologists have discovered many interesting facts about dinosaurs. Paleontologists are scientists who study fossils. Fossils are bones, teeth, and footprints from the past.

Nowadays, about six new kinds of dinosaurs are discovered every year. Paleontologists are also learning more about the dinosaurs whose bones are already displayed in museums—and sometimes they change their ideas about some of these dinosaurs. Each new fossil discovery adds another clue to the mystery story of these amazing creatures from the ancient past.

Suppose you could travel back in time . . . these are just a few of the more remarkable dinosaurs you might meet:

**The Biggest Dinosaur:** A few dinosaurs could compete for this title. *Seismosaurus,* 128 to 170 feet long, was half the length of a football field. It was discovered in 1986 and may be the longest of all dinosaurs. Scientists have also found a couple of bones from two other gigantic plant-eaters: *Supersaurus,* 98 feet long, was as tall as a five-story building. *Ultrasauros,* about 100 feet long, was as tall as a six-story building. Were these the tallest dinosaurs of all—or are these bones really from a tall *Brachiosaurus?* Next year maybe scientists will discover an even bigger dinosaur!

**The Fiercest Dinosaur:** When you think of the most terrifying dinosaur, you probably think first of *Tyrannosaurus rex.* That's because you never met *Utahraptor,* a vicious dinosaur found in Utah in 1991. Nicknamed "superslasher," this small but deadly animal had a fifteen-inch killer claw on each foot. Swift and smart, a pack of hungry *Utahraptors* could easily slaughter a huge plant-eater.

**The Earliest Dinosaur:** *Eoraptor* was only the size of a sheep and ran on two legs. In 1991, in Argentina, paleontologists found the well-preserved skeleton of this meat-eater. It looked like a small version of *Tyrannosaurus rex.* Scientists who studied its primitive jaw, teeth, and bone structure believe that *Eoraptor* lived 228 million years ago and was an ancestor of hundreds of kinds of dinosaurs that came later.

# Life on Earth

A long, long time ago, more than four and a half billion years ago, there was no planet Earth. It's hard to even imagine, but there was just dust, gases, and bits of rocks swirling around in space. Slowly they all came together and began to form this planet.

When the earth was born there were no trees or grass or living creatures of any kind. Finally, after another billion years, the first simple forms of life began to grow.

How do we know so much about things that happened so very long ago? Scientists called geologists study our earth. They can examine the rocks on the earth today and learn about our planet's past.

The Precambrian era lasted four billion years. During this time, the earth was formed and the first signs of life began to appear in the seas. Some of the earliest creatures were soft jellyfish and worms.

Geologists have divided the earth's long history into four different periods, or eras. The earth was formed in the **Precambrian** era. At first the earth was just a ball of hot liquid rock. Over the next several million years it began to cool off, and as it cooled, a crust of hard rock formed on the outside of the ball. Steam rose up and made clouds, and the clouds poured down rain for thousands of years, creating oceans, lakes, and rivers.

The first creatures that grew in the seas were tiny— microscopic algae and bacteria, each just a single cell. Scientists don't know too much about these creatures because they were soft, with no shells or bones, so they didn't leave any fossils for people to study. (You can read about fossils on page 12.) These simple forms of life evolved over many years into larger and more complicated kinds of creatures, like jellyfish and worms.

In the Paleozoic era, life on earth evolved from simple, soft-bodied sea creatures to amphibians that could live on dry land. Paleozoic means "ancient life."

In the 160 million years of the Mesozoic era, dinosaurs evolved, ruled the earth, and became extinct. Mesozoic means "middle life."

The **Paleozoic** era began 600 million years ago. At first, much of the earth was covered with water, and many new kinds of sea creatures evolved. Some of the first creatures with hard skins, or shells, were called trilobites and brachiopods (shellfish). All of these were invertebrates—animals with no backbone or skeleton inside. The seas were also full of corals, sponges, and snails, creatures we still find in our oceans today. Next came the first fish that were vertebrates, which means they had a skeleton inside, instead of a hard shell outside. As millions of years passed, large armored sea creatures with horny shells developed.

They were similar to present-day crabs. On dry land the first plants with stalks and leaves started to grow. Many other kinds of fish evolved, and one new kind of creature, called amphibians, lived partly in water and partly on land. Amphibians could crawl on their fleshy fins and could breathe oxygen from the air. Over the next forty million years, these amphibians lived in the swamplands covered by giant ferns, eating enormous dragonflies and other insects. But they still went back to the sea to lay their eggs. In the next stage of history, the amphibians evolved into many different species that could live on dry land.

In the **Mesozoic** era reptiles ruled the earth and evolved into many different types of animals, including dinosaurs. The Mesozoic era is divided into three periods: in the *Triassic* period, much of the earth was a desert; tree ferns and pine trees grew. Many kinds of creatures continued to evolve on dry land, while other reptiles returned to the oceans, and others even became able to fly. The most spectacular reptiles were the dinosaurs, which ruled the earth during the *Jurassic* period. At the same time, some reptiles were evolving into birds. In the *Cretaceous* period, the climate was moist. The dinosaurs became extinct. This means that they all died, so there are no more dinosaurs alive on our earth. But we do have other creatures from that era in our world today, including turtles and crocodiles, lizards and snakes.

The **Cenozoic** era, the Age of Mammals, began 65 million years ago and continues into our present time. Many, many changes took place in the types of creatures living upon our earth. The number of small mammals grew, and over the next several million years they lived all over the planet. The earliest whales appeared in the seas, and bats flew in the air along with many kinds of birds. Monkeys evolved in the dense forests of the earth, and the larger birds that could not fly became extinct. Over time, the earth's weather became much cooler, and the forests shrank as the plains and prairies grew in size. Modern humans began to evolve about two and a half million years ago.

The last couple of million years of the Cenozoic era are sometimes called the Age of Man. In those years there were periods of very cold weather, known as Ice Ages, alternating with times of warmer weather. The earliest humans hunted large mammals, lived in caves or huts, and used tools made of stone. As the enormous walls of ice known as glaciers melted, human beings began to farm the land and to tame animals to help with the work.

The history of the world before anything was written down is called prehistory. Prehistoric time ended about 5,000 years ago, when humans began to use written symbols.

Cenozoic means "modern life." The Cenozoic era includes the most recent 65 million years of history. It began as the Age of Mammals, and we live today in the Age of Man.

# A changing world

Our planet Earth is not a solid ball of rock. The outside crust, on which we live, is split into pieces, called plates. All the continents and the ocean floors sit on separate plates of rock. Deep underneath the crust is a thick layer of very hot melted rock, called magma. The plates of rock float on this magma layer. Because the magma is liquid, it can move and change shape. When it does, the floating outer crust moves, too. This causes earthquakes and volcanoes.

anywhere, because there were no oceans in between to stop them. This explains why today scientists can find fossils of the same kinds of animals all over the world, even in places that are now divided by large oceans. Some Triassic dinosaurs were *Eoraptor, Coelophysis,* and *Plateosaurus.*

**Jurassic World**
**190-135 million years ago**
Late in the Jurassic period, Pangaea began to divide into two parts: Laurasia in the north, and Gondwanaland in the south. By the end of the Jurassic period, dinosaurs were living all over the earth and the two land masses had completely split. The northern section made up what would later become the continents of North America, Europe, and Asia; and the southern land mass included South America and Africa. *Apatosaurus* and *Stegosaurus* lived in the Jurassic period.

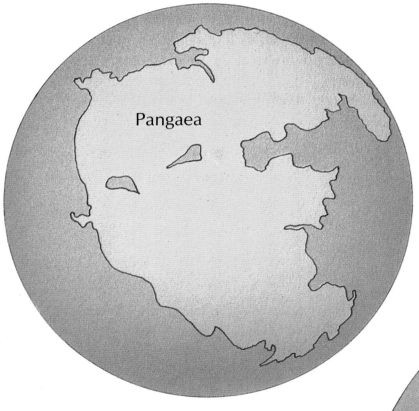

Triassic

**Triassic World**
**225-190 million years ago**
The first dinosaurs lived about 225 million years ago. Back then the earth had no separate continents. Instead there was just one gigantic block of land that geologists call Pangaea.

The animals that lived on Pangaea could travel and live

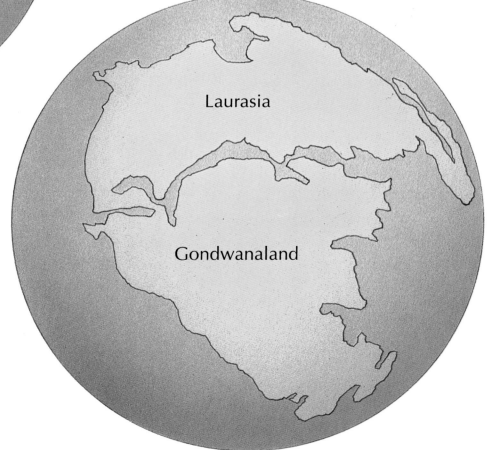

Jurassic

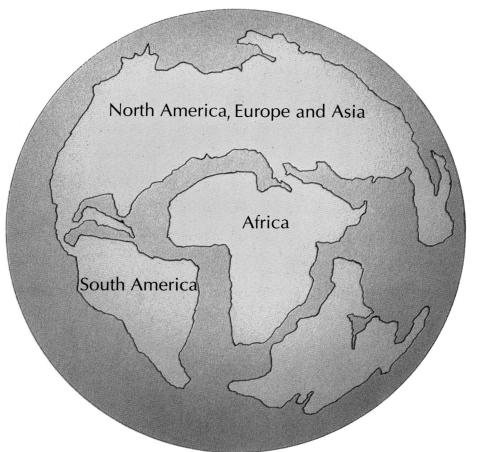

North America, Europe and Asia

Africa

South America

Early Cretaceous

Our earth today is very different from the land where the dinosaurs lived. The continents were not always where they are now.

North America

Asia

Africa

India

South America

Australia

Antarctica

Late Cretaceous

**Early Cretaceous World**
**135-100 million years ago**
As the plates of the earth's crust continued to move, Laurasia and Gondwanaland broke into more pieces. Oceans came between the pieces of land and pushed them farther apart. *Baryonyx* and *Brachiosaurus* were alive at this time.

**Late Cretaceous World**
**100-65 million years ago**
The land split even more, into the continents we know today. Then they slowly began to drift apart. South America split off from Africa, and India started to move back toward Asia. *Tyrannosaurus rex* ruled the Late Cretaceous world.

The continents reached the positions they are in today about 64 million years ago, after the dinosaurs became extinct. India was shoved against the continent of Asia, forming the Himalayan mountains.

The plates of the earth's crust are always being forced apart or pushed together. Over many millions of years, this powerful pushing and pulling has slowly shaped our continents and mountains and oceans. Even now, the earth is still changing. The plates move our continents a tiny bit each year.

# When and where dinosaurs lived

The first reports of the discovery of
dinosaurs date back to the 1820s.

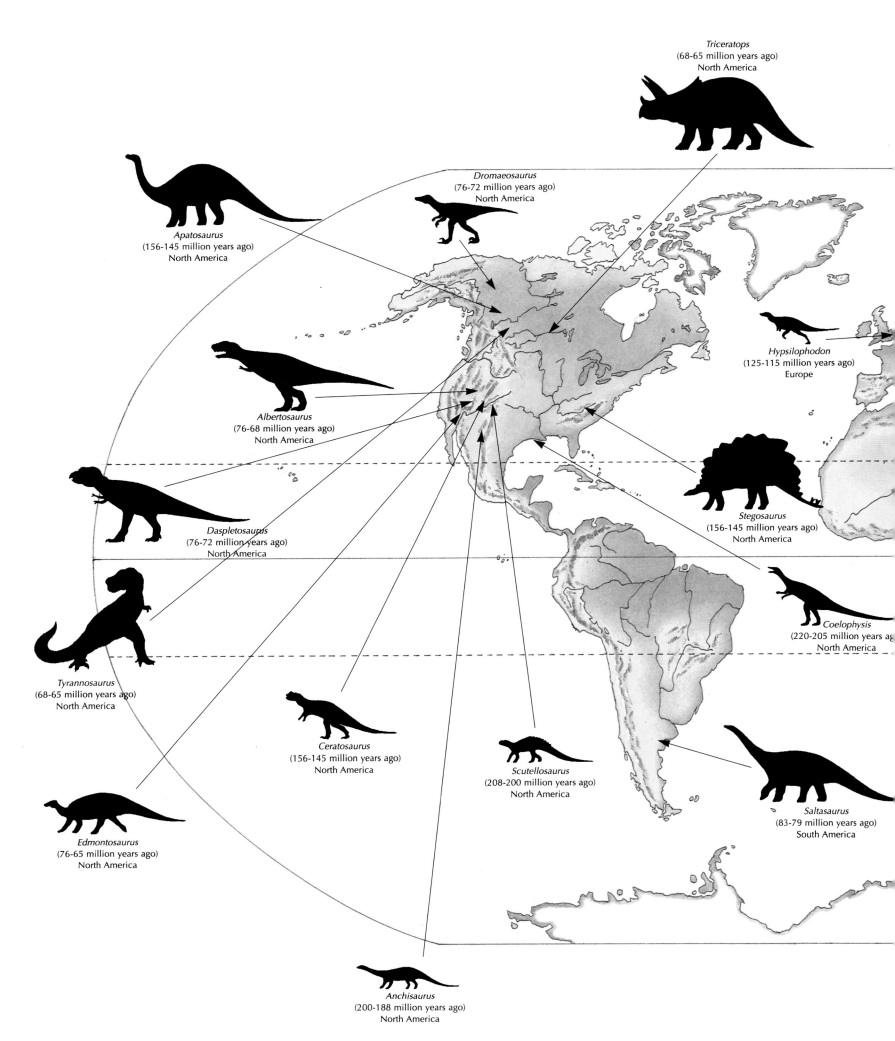

Triceratops
(68-65 million years ago)
North America

Dromaeosaurus
(76-72 million years ago)
North America

Apatosaurus
(156-145 million years ago)
North America

Hypsilophodon
(125-115 million years ago)
Europe

Albertosaurus
(76-68 million years ago)
North America

Stegosaurus
(156-145 million years ago)
North America

Daspletosaurus
(76-72 million years ago)
North America

Coelophysis
(220-205 million years ag
North America

Tyrannosaurus
(68-65 million years ago)
North America

Ceratosaurus
(156-145 million years ago)
North America

Scutellosaurus
(208-200 million years ago)
North America

Saltasaurus
(83-79 million years ago)
South America

Edmontosaurus
(76-65 million years ago)
North America

Anchisaurus
(200-188 million years ago)
North America

Since then the fossilized remains of these prehistoric reptiles have been found all over the world. This map shows where dinosaur fossils have been discovered.

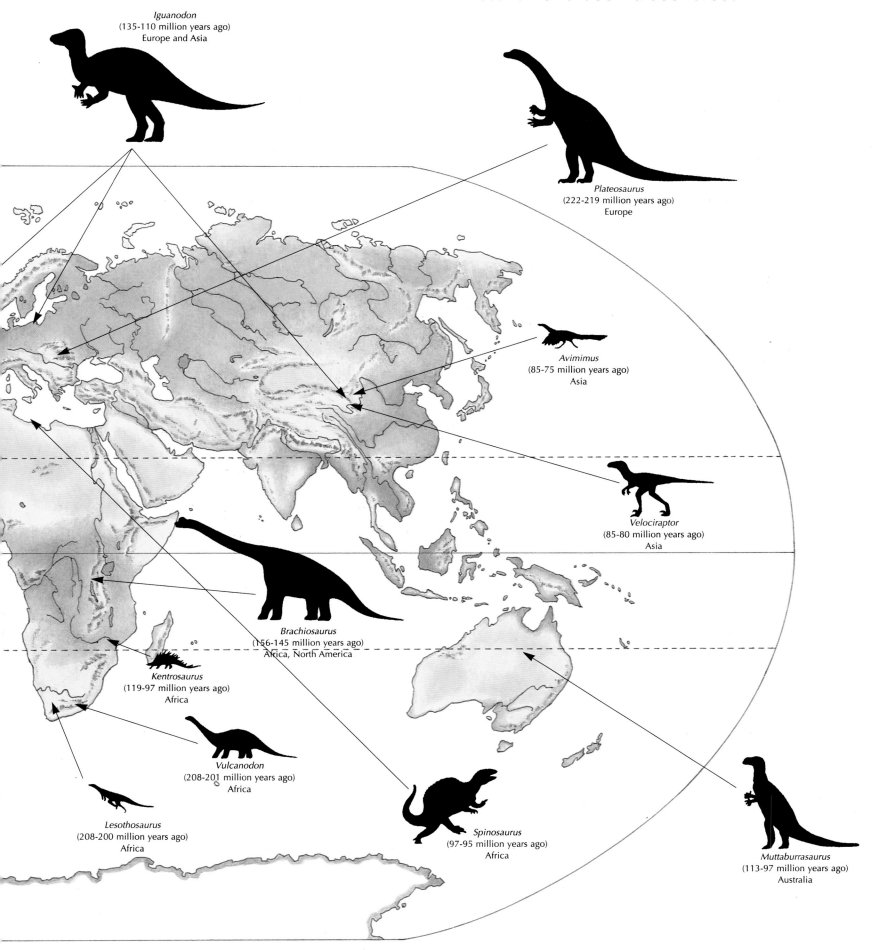

*Iguanodon*
(135-110 million years ago)
Europe and Asia

*Plateosaurus*
(222-219 million years ago)
Europe

*Avimimus*
(85-75 million years ago)
Asia

*Velociraptor*
(85-80 million years ago)
Asia

*Brachiosaurus*
(156-145 million years ago)
Africa, North America

*Kentrosaurus*
(119-97 million years ago)
Africa

*Vulcanodon*
(208-201 million years ago)
Africa

*Lesothosaurus*
(208-200 million years ago)
Africa

*Spinosaurus*
(97-95 million years ago)
Africa

*Muttaburrasaurus*
(113-97 million years ago)
Australia

11

# What were dinosaurs like?

Dinosaurs came in many shapes and sizes. Some had scales like snakes; others had armor like crocodiles. And a few may have had feathers like birds! Some dinosaurs were herbivores, which means they ate only plants; some were carnivores and ate the flesh of other animals; and still others were omnivores—they ate both plants and animals. Scientists believe that some dinosaurs were warm-blooded. This means their bodies kept a steady warm temperature that gave them energy to run far and fast. All the reptiles alive today are cold-blooded. They must lie in the sun to get warmth and energy.

Scientists discover more about dinosaurs every year, but there are many things we will never know. For example, what color were they? This is something that scientists cannot tell from the fossils of these ancient creatures.

One thing we are sure of is that dinosaurs lived on land, even though they probably wandered into marshy areas. Like today's reptiles they breathed air with lungs, and their babies hatched from eggs.

How do scientists know so much about dinosaurs? They study fossils to learn what life was like long, long ago. A fossil is a bone or a tooth or a footprint that has, over many years, turned to stone. Fossils are clues to the ancient past. Let's say a dinosaur died suddenly in a swampy area. Instead of decomposing, or rotting, its body sank into the mud and stayed there for millions of years, while above, on the surface of the earth, everything changed—the swamp

dried out and earth, sand, and bits of rock piled up in many thick, heavy layers on top of the dinosaur. The hard parts of the dinosaur's body (its bones, teeth, and scales), turned into stony fossils.

This process takes thousands of years. In the same way fossils preserve the harder parts of plants (the seeds and pollen), or the skeletons of the earliest human beings, and even footprints left on soft soil. Millions of years later, as the surface of the earth continues to change, fossils are discovered, sometimes by accident, sometimes on purpose. The weather can help—for example, the wind blows sand around in the desert and may uncover hidden layers of fossils; or a river may wash up long-buried layers of earth. Other fossils are found by paleontologists digging in search of clues to the past.

Paleontologists can tell how big or how small a dinosaur was by the size of its bones. From the jaws and teeth they can figure out what a dinosaur ate. Meat-eaters, for example, needed strong, sharp teeth. From the shape of parts of the skull, they can guess how smart a dinosaur was, and how well it could see or hear or smell. Fossilized footprints tell about a dinosaur's size and weight, and how it walked or ran.

# The first dinosaurs

Ancient reptiles were the ancestors of all dinosaurs, birds, and even mammals. One ancient group of reptiles was the Thecodonts. Some Thecodonts developed straight back legs that kept their bodies upright. All the other reptiles crawled with their bellies close to the ground. About 225 million years ago the Thecodonts evolved into dinosaurs. The first dinosaurs were small animals, only about three feet long. They ran on their hind legs. The earliest dinosaur we know about is *Eoraptor,* which looked like a small *Tyrannosaurus rex.*

*Plateosaurus* was one of the first large plant-eaters. It was twenty-seven feet long and weighed 1,500 pounds. *Plateosaurus* had thumb claws which it may have used to grab its food or to fight off its enemies.

One of the oldest and most primitive dinosaurs was *Coelophysis,* a small, thin meat-eater with sharp teeth. It could run fast on two or four legs, and some scientists think it may have been warm-blooded.

*Coelophysis*

220 million years ago

210 million years ago

200 mi

*Massospondylus,* a smaller relative of *Plateosaurus,* was twelve to twenty feet long and also ate plants. It had strong back legs and arms and huge, clawed thumbs.

*Dilophosaurus* is the oldest known large meat-eating dinosaur. It had a double crest on its head and a slim but strong body. Its teeth were sharp for tearing the flesh of other animals.

*Plateosaurus*

*Dilophosaurus*

*Massospondylus*

*Anchisaurus*

*Anchisaurus* was the first dinosaur discovered in North America. It was only about eight feet long. When scientists noticed its blunt, rounded teeth, they decided *Anchisaurus* may have been one of the very first dinosaurs to eat plants as well as meat.

ars ago

190 million years ago

180 million years ago

# Saurischians and Ornithischians

When the first dinosaur bones were discovered many years ago, no one knew what they were. As scientists studied some of these enormous, strange bones, they realized that they were not from any creature anyone had ever seen. In 1841, Richard Owen, a famous English scientist, named them "dinosaurs," which comes from the Greek words for "terrible lizard." Forty-six years later, after many fossils had been discovered and carefully studied, scientists realized that "dinosaurs" were really two different types of animals, so they divided them into two groups, named Saurischians and Ornithischians.  Saurischian means "lizard-hipped," and Ornithischian means "bird-hipped." The bones of their hips were different shapes and they pointed in different directions. The difference in their hips made these two groups of dinosaurs stand and move differently.

Ornithischians

Saurischians

**Saurischians**

The two lower hip bones of these dinosaurs were separate and pointed in different directions. The long, thin pubic bone was in line with the back legs. This "lizard-hipped" group includes three types of dinosaurs. The first, the Theropods, all had short necks and big heads; they stood on two legs and ate meat. The Sauropods were gigantic plant-eaters with long necks and small heads. Most of the Prosauropods were plant-eaters, but some of them ate meat.

**Ornithischians**

The two lower hip bones of the dinosaurs in this group were close together and pointed backward, lining up with the bone of the hind leg. The "bird-hipped" group includes all the other plant-eaters—the Stegosaurs (plated dinosaurs), the Ankylosaurs (armored dinosaurs), the Ceratopsians (horned dinosaurs), and the Ornithopods (some of which were duck-billed).

# Carnivorous dinosaurs

All the carnivorous, or meat-eating, dinosaurs were in the group called Theropods, which means "with the feet of wild beasts." These "lizard-hipped" dinosaurs walked on two legs, and their small front legs had very sharp claws. Their powerful jaws could tear chunks of flesh from the bodies of other animals. Some Theropods were big and some were small, but they all had strong hind legs for traveling over the hard earth of the plains where they hunted for food.

Carnosaurs were large and heavily built dinosaurs. The best known is *Tyrannosaurus rex,* one of the most vicious and terrifying creatures that has ever walked the earth. It was the size of a large truck and was incredibly strong. Its saw-edged teeth were six inches long. *Tyrannosaurus* could run very fast when it wanted to, using its whiplike tail for balance. But this killer didn't always hunt, sometimes finding it easier to eat the flesh of dead animals that it found on the ground.

*Velociraptor* was about the size of a wolf. The arched claws on its front legs served as deadly weapons.

*Allosaurus* was big and powerful. Its jaws were lined with razor-sharp teeth that curved backward. Its long tail was used to balance its tremendous weight, which could reach up to one and a half tons—three thousand pounds!

*Tarbosaurus* was one of the last dinosaurs on earth. This forty-five-foot-long creature was almost identical to *Tyrannosaurus rex* except that it was lighter and had a larger head.

*Albertosaurus* was heavily built, with a large head, a short body, and a long, powerful tail. Each of its front legs had just two claws.

*Ceratosaurus,* which means "horned lizard," had two bony, hornlike shapes above its eyes. It had huge, sharp fangs and was about twenty feet long.

19

# Deinonychus

In 1964, in the clay soil of Montana, paleontologists made an exciting discovery. They found a whole graveyard of dinosaurs all of the same type—and some were full skeletons. The scientists named this animal *Deinonychus,* which means "terrible claw," because of the fearsome claw on one of the toes of its hind feet. Before they discovered *Deinonychus,* scientists believed that all dinosaurs were stupid and slow and cold-blooded. But they could tell from its bones that *Deinonychus* was different—fast, nimble, and intelligent. And it seemed to have been a warm-blooded animal!

Deinonychus was a fierce hunter that would attack animals much larger than itself—gigantic Sauropods and even Ankylosaurs, whose bodies were protected by plates of bony armor. Like lions, wolves, or other modern predators, Deinonychus hunted in packs: together these dinosaurs would attack a young, old, or sick animal. One of their favorite victims may have been Tenontosaurus. This dinosaur was ten times larger and heavier than a single Deinonychus, but it was a very slow-moving creature with an unprotected belly.

Deinonychus was about ten feet long and six feet high. It had more than seventy saw-edged teeth that were perfect for ripping flesh. Few animals could hope to escape from its powerful bite.

The most unusual feature of Deinonychus was its hind leg with the large, curved claw. When it ran—and it could run very fast—it used its first toe for balance and kept its enormous curved claw raised and ready to strike its prey. This five-inch claw was a deadly weapon that cut and slashed the victim's flesh without mercy.

# Large herbivores

Many dinosaurs were herbivores, which means they ate only plants. One group, the Sauropods, grew astonishingly huge. These dinosaurs needed enormous stomachs to digest the rough fiber of the plants they ate. They swallowed the more tender leaves of ferns and other plants without chewing them. They also ate the tougher leaves of conifers, cycads, magnolias, and oaks. Then they would swallow rough stones and pine cones. These stones and pine cones rubbed together in their stomachs to grind their food into a soft vegetable mass. Today, in a similar way, birds swallow small stones to grind the food inside their stomachs.

The many varieties of ferns were the favorite food of the herbivores.

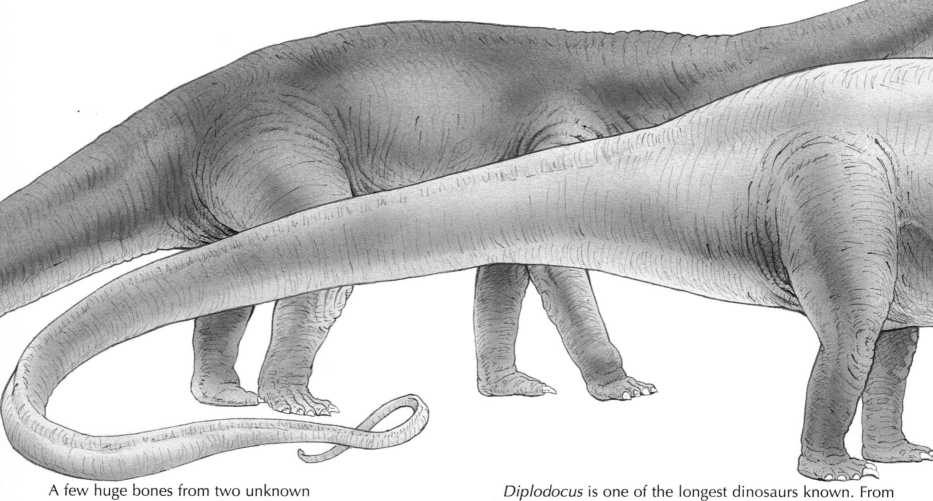

A few huge bones from two unknown Sauropods were found in Colorado in the 1970s. These two dinosaurs have been named *Supersaurus* and *Ultrasauros.* Their shoulder bones were more than eight feet long! Scientists still do not know too much about these dinosaurs. It may even be that these are just the bones of a big *Brachiosaurus.*

*Diplodocus* is one of the longest dinosaurs known. From nose to tail it measured about ninety feet, but most of its length was its long neck and whiplike tail. Some scientists think *Seismosaurus* may have been even longer. *Seismosaurus* looked very much like *Diplodocus.*

Cycads were the ancestors of palm trees.

Even in prehistoric times, large forests of tall conifers—pine trees—grew in hilly areas.

One of the longest necks of any known animal belonged to *Mamenchisaurus.* With its thirty-six-foot neck, it could eat plants that other herbivores couldn't even reach.

The enormous *Apatosaurus* was once known as *Brontosaurus,* the "thunder lizard," because when it moved around with its thirty-three tons of weight it must have made a huge noise, like the rumbling of thunder. Like *Diplodocus, Apatosaurus* raised itself on its back legs to reach the tender leaves at the treetops. It could also use its great weight to protect itself from other dinosaurs. When a meat-eater attacked, it could rear up and plunge down to crush its enemy.

# Armored dinosaurs

Ankylosaurs were a group of armored dinosaurs. These four-legged plant-eaters had squat, heavy bodies. Their necks, backs, sides, and tails were covered with bony armor that was as thick as leather. This armor consisted of an assortment of plates, horns, and bony knobs joined together and firmly attached to their skin.

The sheer size of the Ankylosaurs made them frightening animals. They sometimes weighed several tons and could be up to thirty feet long. Even though the heavy Ankylosaurs moved slowly, a hungry carnivore wouldn't have much luck attacking one of these heavily armored dinosaurs. An Ankylosaur's one weak area was its soft, unarmored belly, but when it sensed danger, *Ankylosaurus* would lie down on the ground and protect itself with its thick spiny back. Even the mighty *Tyrannosaurus* was not strong enough to roll an *Ankylosaurus* over to attack its soft belly.

*Ankylosaurus* was the largest Ankylosaur and one of the last dinosaurs to live on the earth. Its large, sturdy body was covered with thick bands of armor that reached its tail. At the end of the tail was a huge bony lump that it could swing like a club to strike its enemies.

The armored head of *Talarurus* had two pairs of pointed horns. The barrel-shaped body was protected with thick armor plates and other rows of spikes, especially on the sides. Its strong clubbed tail made an excellent weapon.

*Kentrosaurus* was a large dinosaur, sixteen feet long and very similar to *Stegosaurus.* It had a double row of narrow triangular plates along its back and eight pairs of tall spikes running down its tail.

*Panoplosaurus* was smaller than the other Ankylosaurs but had the same thickset build and bony armor, with square plates arranged across its neck and shoulders. The row of sharp spikes on each side made it almost impossible to attack. Its huge, pear-shaped head was fully protected by thick plates.

# Stegosaurus

*Stegosaurus* lived some 150 million years ago. It was about the size of an elephant—twenty-five feet long and weighing about two tons—yet it had a brain that was only the size of a walnut! Its large back legs were twice as big as its front legs, so *Stegosaurus* was very slow and clumsy and walked with its small head near the ground. This dinosaur is best known for the bony triangular plates that ran down its back and along its tail. Some of them were as much as thirty inches high.

This plant-eating dinosaur had a tremendous appetite. It ate more than 600 pounds of plants every day. It couldn't chew all this food, because its mouth had no teeth in front and only a few bony knobs, like molars, in the back. Instead, *Stegosaurus* swallowed stones to mash up all the food inside its stomach.

*Stegosaurus* had the smallest brain of all the dinosaurs.

When the first fossilized skeletons of *Stegosaurus* were discovered, the bony triangles were no longer attached and scientists were not sure how to arrange them on the skeleton. At first they thought the plates had been flat against the skin, so they named this animal *Stegosaurus,* which means the "roofed lizard." Later scientists decided the plates stood up along the dinosaur's spine.

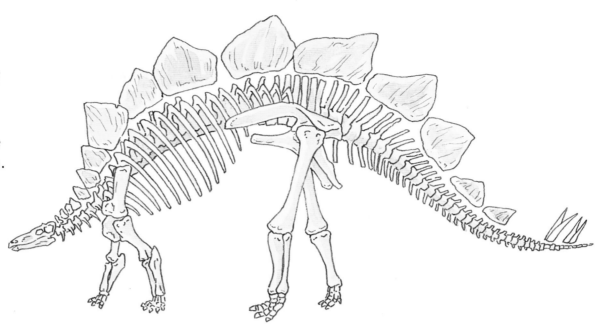

Why did the *Stegosaurus* have these bony triangles? At first most scientists thought they were for protection from the meat-eaters. Other scientists disagreed, noticing that the plates were not very sharply pointed and may not even have been rigid, since they were attached to the dinosaur's skin and not to its bones. Modern scientists have suggested that the plates acted like radiators to control the animal's body temperature. The plates could have absorbed heat from the sun and sent it on to other parts of the big creature's body.

The tail was armed with two pairs of spikes, each twenty inches long. When enemies threatened, *Stegosaurus* could fling its tail around like a whip.

# Horns, collars, and crests

Two groups of plant-eaters are known for the amazing decorations on their heads, which made them look as if they wére wearing fancy hats and collars. The Ceratopsians ("horned lizards") had horns and collars. The Hadrosaurs were "duck-billed" dinosaurs whose heads were covered with bumps, crests, and spikes.

Did these unusual-looking heads and necks help the dinosaurs in some way to survive? Plant-eaters needed protection against the ferocious meat-eaters that were always ready to strike. Perhaps when a meat-eater saw those thick collars and sharp spikes, it might have decided to look elsewhere for its dinner! Scientists have several ideas about the hatlike crests on some dinosaurs' heads: Maybe the crests were used for making sounds to "talk" with other dinosaurs in their herd. Or the crests might have given the dinosaurs a better sense of smell. It is even possible that the crests helped the dinosaurs to recognize their friends.

The collar of *Eucentrosaurus* was edged with spines.

*Triceratops* means "face with three horns."

With its eight-foot collar, *Torosaurus* (the "bull lizard") had the longest head of any land animal that has ever lived.

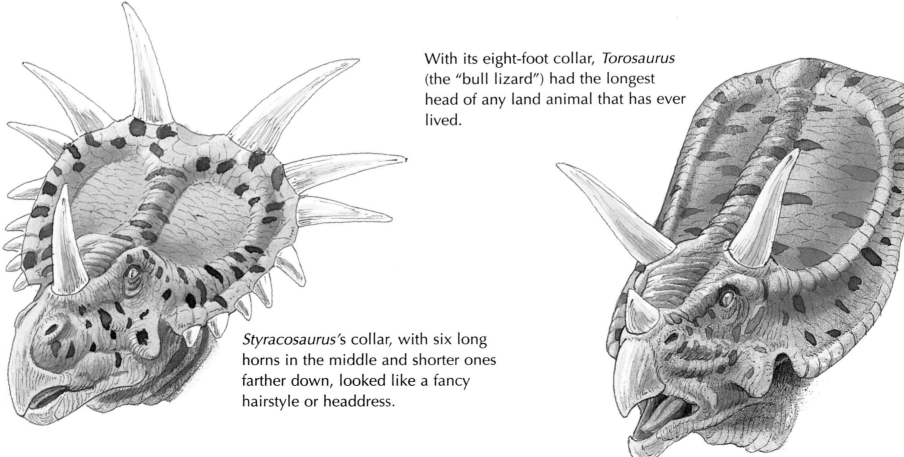

*Styracosaurus's* collar, with six long horns in the middle and shorter ones farther down, looked like a fancy hairstyle or headdress.

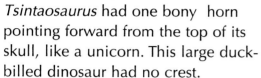

*Tsintaosaurus* had one bony horn pointing forward from the top of its skull, like a unicorn. This large duck-billed dinosaur had no crest.

The hollow crest on the head of *Parasaurolophus* was sometimes two feet long! It may have been used to make sounds or to help the animal push through thick plants.

*Corythosaurus,* the "helmet lizard," had a crest shaped like a helmet. This crest was formed by its nose bones, which stretched up over its head.

The head of *Euoplocephalus* was well protected by a double pair of spines. This animal was fully armored. Even its eyelids were guarded by plates that could be lowered to defend its eyes.

*Saurolophus* had a bony, horn-shaped crest just behind its eyes. It may have been a frame for some skin that could be inflated like a balloon to make honking noises or bellowing sounds.

# Baryonyx

In 1983 scientists in England were very excited by the discovery of a huge, curved claw. This claw was fifteen inches long and seemed to have come from a carnivorous dinosaur. They named this creature *Baryonyx,* which means "heavy claw." Its fossilized bones were embedded in hundreds of tons of rock, and it took many years to find and dig up what remained of the skull and the skeleton. Fossilized fish scales were found near *Baryonyx*'s stomach, and scientists believe it may have used its enormous claw as a kind of harpoon to catch fish, in the same way bears do today. No other dinosaur is known to have eaten fish.

This large, lizard-hipped carnivore may have eaten fish.

The most unusual characteristic of *Baryonyx* was its head. *Allosaurus, Tyrannosaurus,* and the other large meat-eaters all had short, thick heads. But *Baryonyx* had a long, thin head, similar to a crocodile's. With its long curved mouth and thirty-two sharp teeth on each side of its jaw, *Baryonyx,* like the crocodile, had a frightening grin.

# Discovering dinosaurs

Dinosaur bones have been discovered all over the world. Paleontologists hunt for the fossilized bones in places where over millions of years the sand, mud, and layers of dirt have turned into rock.

Paleontologists can do tests to figure out the age of the rock layers and to tell the age of a fossil. Since scientists know that dinosaurs lived 65 to 225 million years ago, they look for dinosaur fossils in the layers of rock that date back to that time.

When digging up a dinosaur, a scientist must be very, very careful. Before any of the fossilized bones are removed from rock, they are photographed, measured, and numbered, and a detailed map is made showing exactly where the bones were discovered. The bones are then hardened with a special chemical so they will not be damaged when they are cut out of the rock. After the fossils have been removed, the sections are each wrapped in foam rubber sheets and packed into strong padded boxes to be taken to a laboratory, where they can be studied more closely.

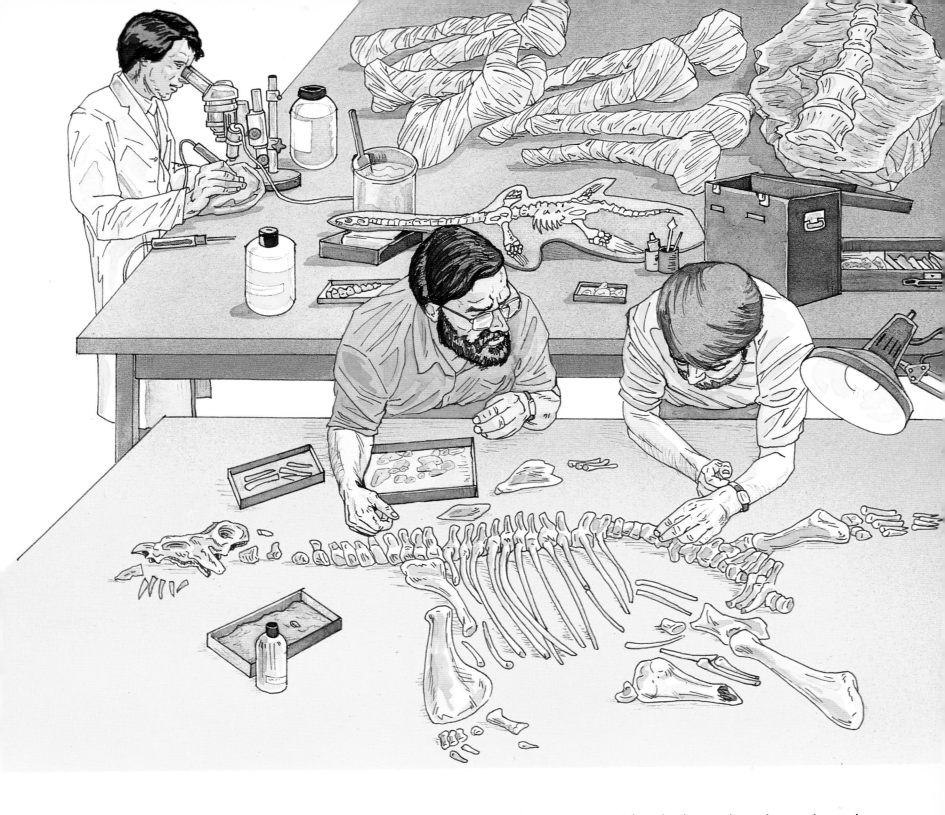

Working in the laboratory may not be quite as exciting—or as tiring—as digging outdoors looking for fossils, but it is just as important. The fossilized bones must be carefully separated from the rocks in which they are embedded. This is done by using small carving tools and light hammers. Skilled technicians use chemicals to dissolve the rocks without harming the fossils. Sometimes they also use sound waves to shake the bones free. Often, to protect themselves from these chemicals, the scientists must wear special clothes and gloves and masks.

After the bones have been cleaned, they are ready to be studied and photographed. Copies of the delicate bones may be made of plaster. The next step is to put together a model, called a reconstruction, of the dinosaur's skeleton.

# Building a dinosaur

Reconstructing a dinosaur is like putting together a complicated puzzle—only you don't have instructions that tell you how the pieces fit together, and you probably don't even have all of the pieces! Building a dinosaur skeleton can take many years of work and study by a whole team of scientists and skilled workers. There are many mysteries: for example, the bones don't tell anything about the soft parts of the animal (its muscle, fat, and skin), which have not been preserved as fossils.

The first step is to put together the main part of the skeleton. This is a very complicated job, even when scientists are working with the bones of an animal they have already studied. Every tiny bit of bone must be put in the right spot. If there is an empty space, is it because a bone is missing, or was soft tissue there when the animal was alive? Scientists usually start by putting together the bones of the pelvis, because this answers some important questions about the dinosaur. Did it, for example, walk on two legs or four? Could it rear up on its back legs? Did it move in an upright position?

The bones also give clues about how the muscles were attached, especially around the hips, shoulders, and head, so scientists can estimate how big the dinosaur was and how it was shaped. Sometimes a bone is found that does not seem to fit anywhere in the skeleton that is being built. This could be a fossil from a different animal, or it might even be a clue to the discovery of a new type of dinosaur—which is every paleontologist's dream!

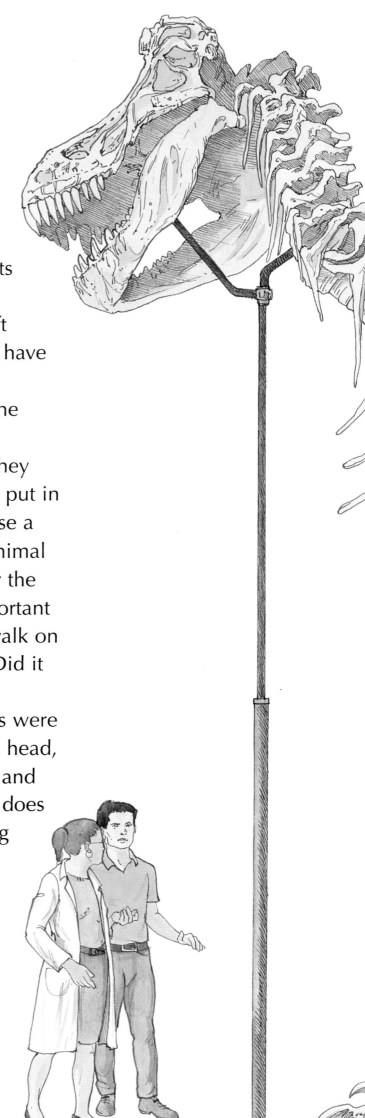

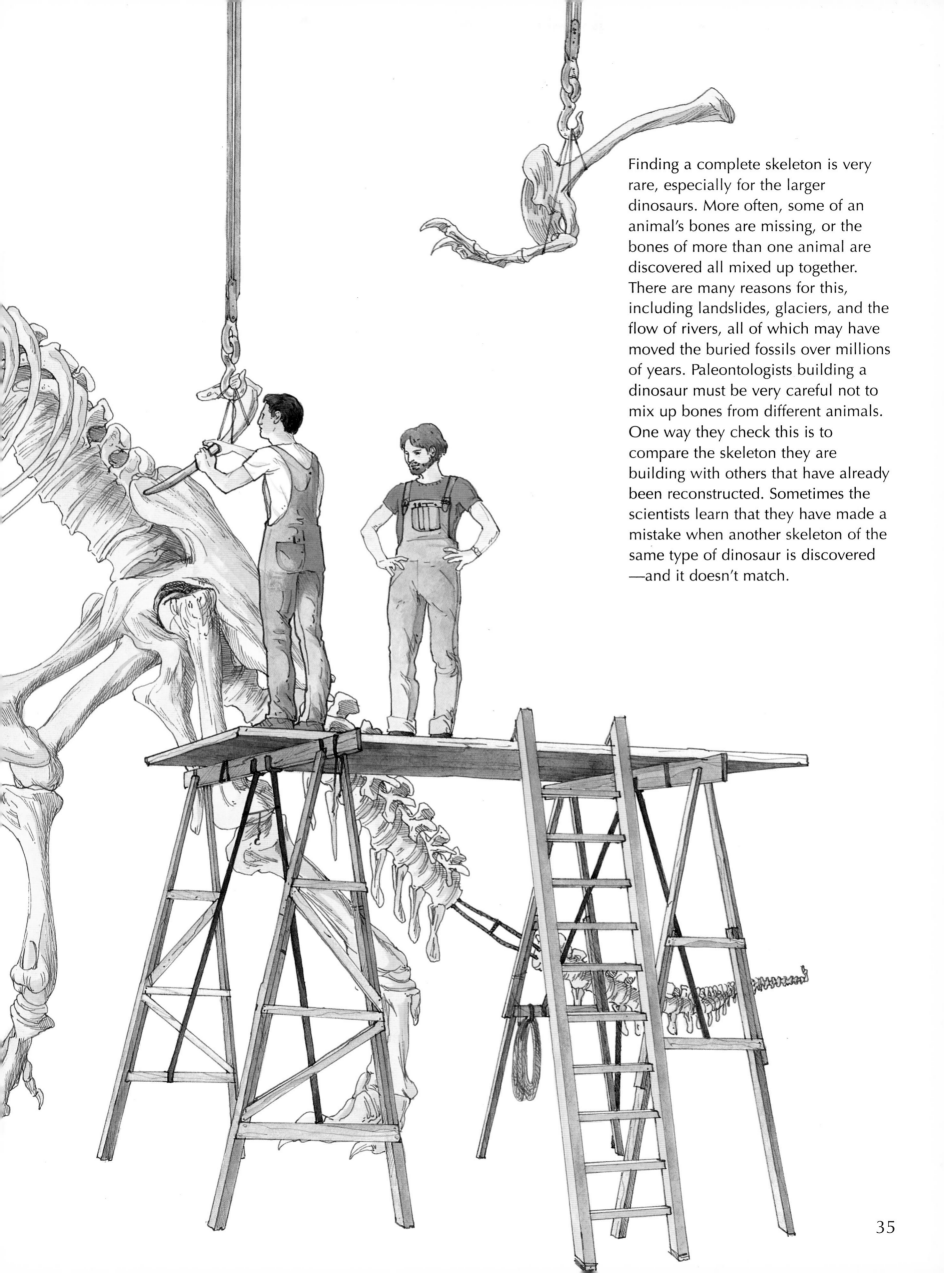

Finding a complete skeleton is very rare, especially for the larger dinosaurs. More often, some of an animal's bones are missing, or the bones of more than one animal are discovered all mixed up together. There are many reasons for this, including landslides, glaciers, and the flow of rivers, all of which may have moved the buried fossils over millions of years. Paleontologists building a dinosaur must be very careful not to mix up bones from different animals. One way they check this is to compare the skeleton they are building with others that have already been reconstructed. Sometimes the scientists learn that they have made a mistake when another skeleton of the same type of dinosaur is discovered —and it doesn't match.

# Eggs, nests, and baby dinosaurs

Like other reptiles and birds, female dinosaurs laid their eggs on dry land, and the eggs were protected by hard shells. This was one of the many ways that dinosaurs were different from their ancestors the amphibians. Amphibians laid their soft-shelled eggs in the water, and when the babies hatched they could easily be eaten by fish.

Because dinosaur eggshells were hard, some eggs became fossilized. These fossilized eggs are very interesting to paleontologists, who have learned many facts from studying the growing baby dinosaurs preserved inside their shells.

Although most adult dinosaurs were huge, their eggs were quite small. If they had been any bigger, the shell would have been too thick to let in enough oxygen to keep the baby dinosaur alive. And bigger eggs might have been too hard for little baby dinosaurs to break when they were ready to hatch. Small and medium-size dinosaurs laid eggs the size of chicken's or turkeys' eggs. The biggest dinosaur egg found was only twice as big as the egg of an ostrich.

The eggs were laid in a hollow in the sand. Maybe the mother dinosaur scooped out a nest with her nose or her feet. The mother would lay about twenty eggs in a nest about six feet wide and three feet deep. Then she would brush some sand over them to protect them from the weather.

Modern reptiles do not stay nearby to protect their eggs or feed their young, but scientists think some dinosaurs were different. They have found some fossilized nests grouped together. Perhaps several mother dinosaurs made nests close to one another so that a few could guard all the eggs while the others went off to look for food.

Dinosaurs are so heavy that scientists do not think they could have sat on their eggs, as birds do. When the eggs hatched, the baby dinosaurs stayed in the nest for only a short time and then went out to explore their surroundings.

# Smaller dinosaurs

When we think of dinosaurs, we usually imagine huge beasts like the giant plant-eaters. But a few kinds of dinosaurs were really very small—no bigger than a hen or a cat. These smaller dinosaurs were fast and graceful runners because they did not have big, heavy bodies to slow them down. Some were meat-eaters and ate insects and little mammals. When they could, they also ate meat from the bodies of animals killed by the bigger carnivores. Other small dinosaurs were plant-eaters and ate the low-growing plants that they could reach.

Scientists have not found many fossils from these small dinosaurs. This is not surprising, for their bones were so little. It's easy to see the huge jaw of a Sauropod lying in the sand, but even an expert fossil hunter might not notice the tiny bones of a very little dinosaur.

Also, not as many fossils exist from the smaller dinosaurs. A dinosaur like *Compsognathus* could be swallowed up by a huge

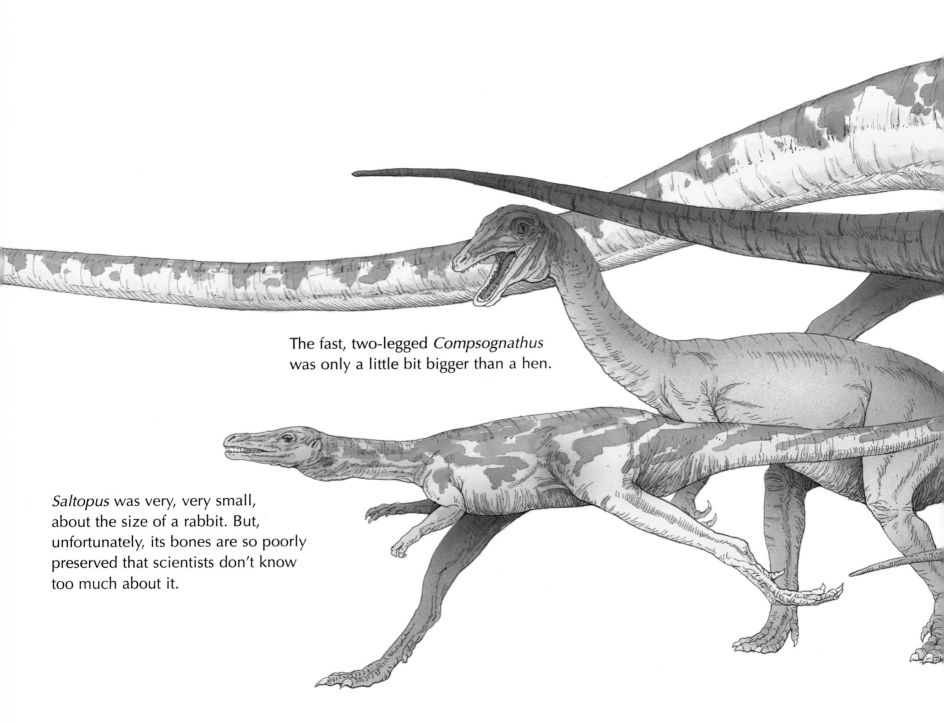

The fast, two-legged *Compsognathus* was only a little bit bigger than a hen.

*Saltopus* was very, very small, about the size of a rabbit. But, unfortunately, its bones are so poorly preserved that scientists don't know too much about it.

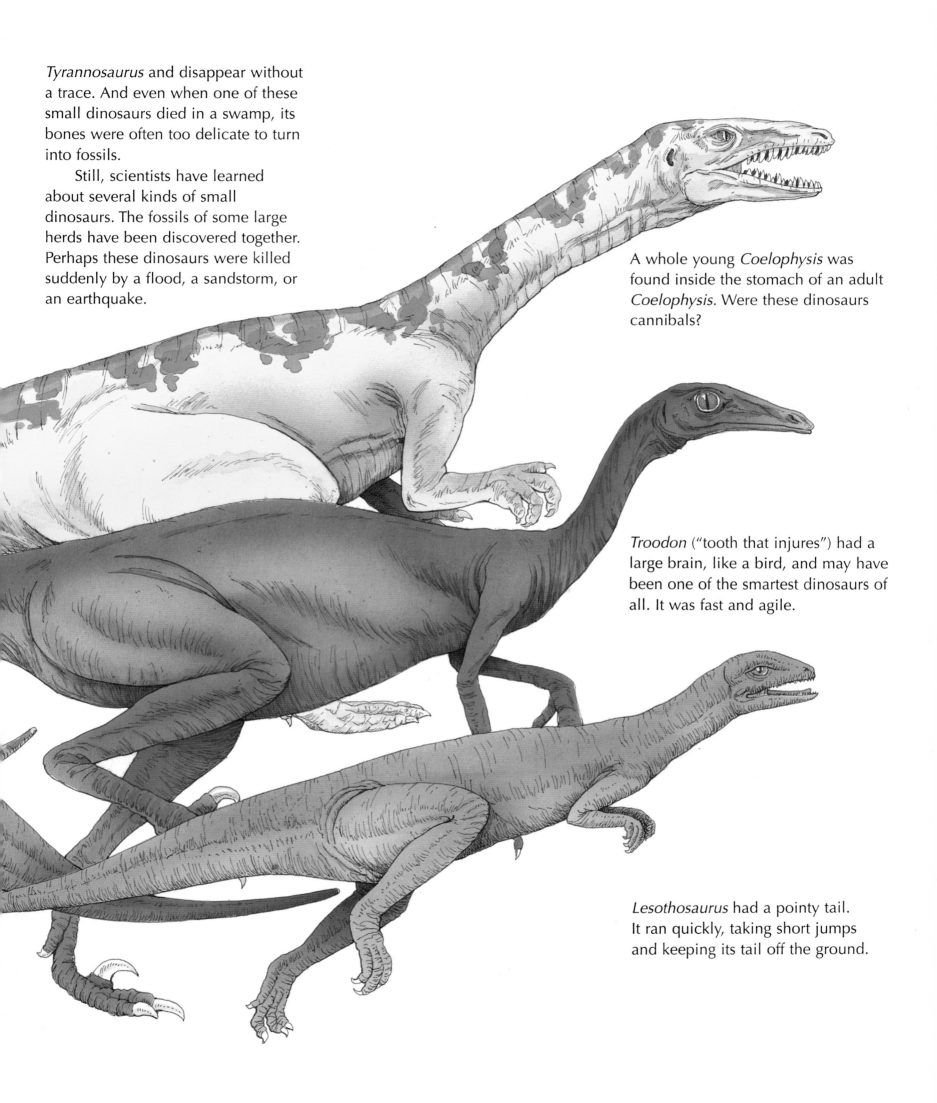

*Tyrannosaurus* and disappear without a trace. And even when one of these small dinosaurs died in a swamp, its bones were often too delicate to turn into fossils.

Still, scientists have learned about several kinds of small dinosaurs. The fossils of some large herds have been discovered together. Perhaps these dinosaurs were killed suddenly by a flood, a sandstorm, or an earthquake.

A whole young *Coelophysis* was found inside the stomach of an adult *Coelophysis*. Were these dinosaurs cannibals?

*Troodon* ("tooth that injures") had a large brain, like a bird, and may have been one of the smartest dinosaurs of all. It was fast and agile.

*Lesothosaurus* had a pointy tail. It ran quickly, taking short jumps and keeping its tail off the ground.

# Egg thief, or caring mother?

The name *Oviraptor* means "egg thief," and since 1923 scientists have believed that Oviraptorids stole and ate the eggs of other dinosaurs. That is because the first *Oviraptor* skeleton that was discovered was lying right on top of a nest of dinosaur eggs in the Gobi Desert. Scientists assumed the eggs were from a *Protoceratops*. It looked as if the *Oviraptor* had been killed by a sudden sandstorm while raiding the nest.

A recent discovery, in 1993, let us peek inside a broken dinosaur egg from a nearby area of the Gobi Desert. This unhatched dinosaur was an Oviraptorid, not a *Protoceratops*. The paleontologist who found the fossilized embryo believes it shows that *Oviraptor* was not an egg thief after all—instead of stealing another dinosaur's eggs, she was just protecting her own!

Each dinosaur discovery brings more questions: Were the eggs found seventy years ago from an *Oviraptor*, like this embryo, or from a *Protoceratops*? Was *Oviraptor* really an egg thief—or just a good parent?

*Oviraptor* had a short head like a parrot, strong toothless jaws, and a horny beak. In other ways *Oviraptor* was like the other Therapods, with muscular arms, long legs, and a long, powerful tail.

40

# Bird imitators

Another unusual group of dinosaurs was called Ornithomimids, which means "bird imitators." The *Struthiomimus,* or "ostrich imitator," had a toothless beak, large eye sockets, long legs, and a slender neck, which made it look like a modern ostrich. With its large eyes *Struthiomimus* could have quickly noticed an enemy coming near. It probably used its strong, long legs to kick its smaller enemies. But when attacked by larger meat-eaters, like a *Deinonychus* pack, it would have had to run its fastest to escape. *Struthiomimus* could run at least twenty-five miles an hour and was one of the fastest dinosaurs.

*Struthiomimus* was a carnivore. Its weak jaws show that it may have eaten eggs or soft-bodied animals. Some scientists used to think that *Struthiomimus* ate plants, too, but modern scientists disagree. With its long neck it probably also snapped up insects, lizards, and small mammals. *Struthiomimus* had large, flexible hands for digging or for cleaning off food.

# Dinosaur tails

Dinosaurs' tails helped the dinosaur in a couple of ways. When another animal attacked, a four-legged dinosaur could swing its tail like a club to protect itself. It could hit the attacker in the front legs and knock it over, or it might aim for the enemy's throat. For a dinosaur standing or running on two legs, the tail was needed to balance the weight of the animal's body.

When meat-eaters attacked, many plant-eaters used their tails to strike back at their enemies. The Stegosaurs' tails were armed with spikes. An Ankylosaur's tail had heavy, bony lumps at the end.

*Ornithomimus* is one of the dinosaurs that used its tail for balance and to help it change direction when it was running incredibly fast.

What would happen if a hungry *Tarbosaurus* (left) wanted to eat this armored *Euoplocephalus?* The powerful *Euoplocephalus* could lie down, protected by its bony armor and big pointy horns. Or it might lash out and defend itself—using its heavy tail with bony knobs.

# Hadrosaurs

Hadrosaur means "bulky lizards." The animals of this group have been nicknamed the "duck-billed dinosaurs" because they all had flat snouts and beaks like today's ducks. Hadrosaurs had heavy bodies and could walk on four legs or on two. When they needed to run away from their enemies, they ran on two legs and used their tails for balance. When they were eating or resting, these plant-eaters stood on all four legs.

Most of the Hadrosaurs had unusual crests and other adornments on their heads. Scientists have used these crests to divide the Hadrosaurs into two groups. The Hadrosaurians had flat heads with solid bony crests, or no crests at all. The Lambaeosaurians had long heads with large, hollow crests on top.

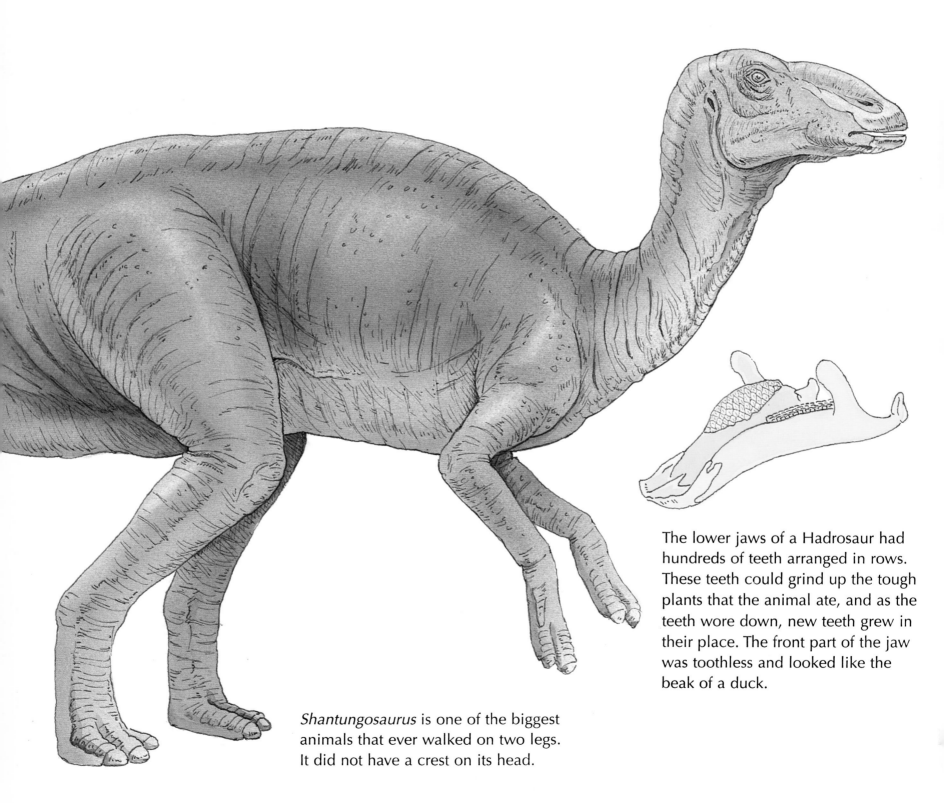

The lower jaws of a Hadrosaur had hundreds of teeth arranged in rows. These teeth could grind up the tough plants that the animal ate, and as the teeth wore down, new teeth grew in their place. The front part of the jaw was toothless and looked like the beak of a duck.

*Shantungosaurus* is one of the biggest animals that ever walked on two legs. It did not have a crest on its head.

*Corythosaurus* was a big dinosaur with a high, fanlike crest. Scientists wonder if it used its crest to make sounds to attract other dinosaurs in its herd or to "talk" to them in some way.

*Saurolophus* had a large head with a solid, hornlike crest at the back. *Parasaurolophus* had an unusual hollow crest. Scientists think that the male *Parasaurolophuses* had longer crests than the females.

*Saurolophus*

*Corythosaurus*

*Parasaurolophus*

45

# Flying lizards

Pterosaurs were the first vertebrates to fly. They were not flying dinosaurs and they were not birds. They were winged reptiles that sailed through the air on flaps of skin that stretched from their front fingers to their back legs. Bats have wings like these.

Pterosaurs lived about 70 million years before the first birds, and they became extinct long before the dinosaurs disappeared from the earth. There were two main groups of Pterosaurs. Rhamphorhynchans were more primitive and had teeth and tails. Pterodactyls were more highly developed and had toothless beaks and shorter tails.

The enormous *Quetzalcoatlus* had very long, narrow wings with a forty-foot wingspan. It was the size of a small airplane! Scientists think it was the largest flying creature that ever existed.

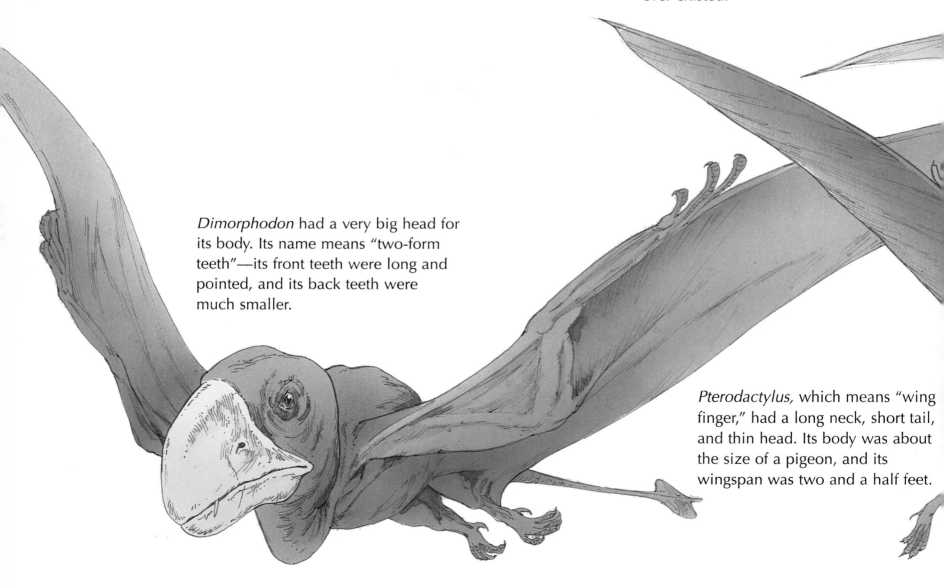

*Dimorphodon* had a very big head for its body. Its name means "two-form teeth"—its front teeth were long and pointed, and its back teeth were much smaller.

*Pterodactylus,* which means "wing finger," had a long neck, short tail, and thin head. Its body was about the size of a pigeon, and its wingspan was two and a half feet.

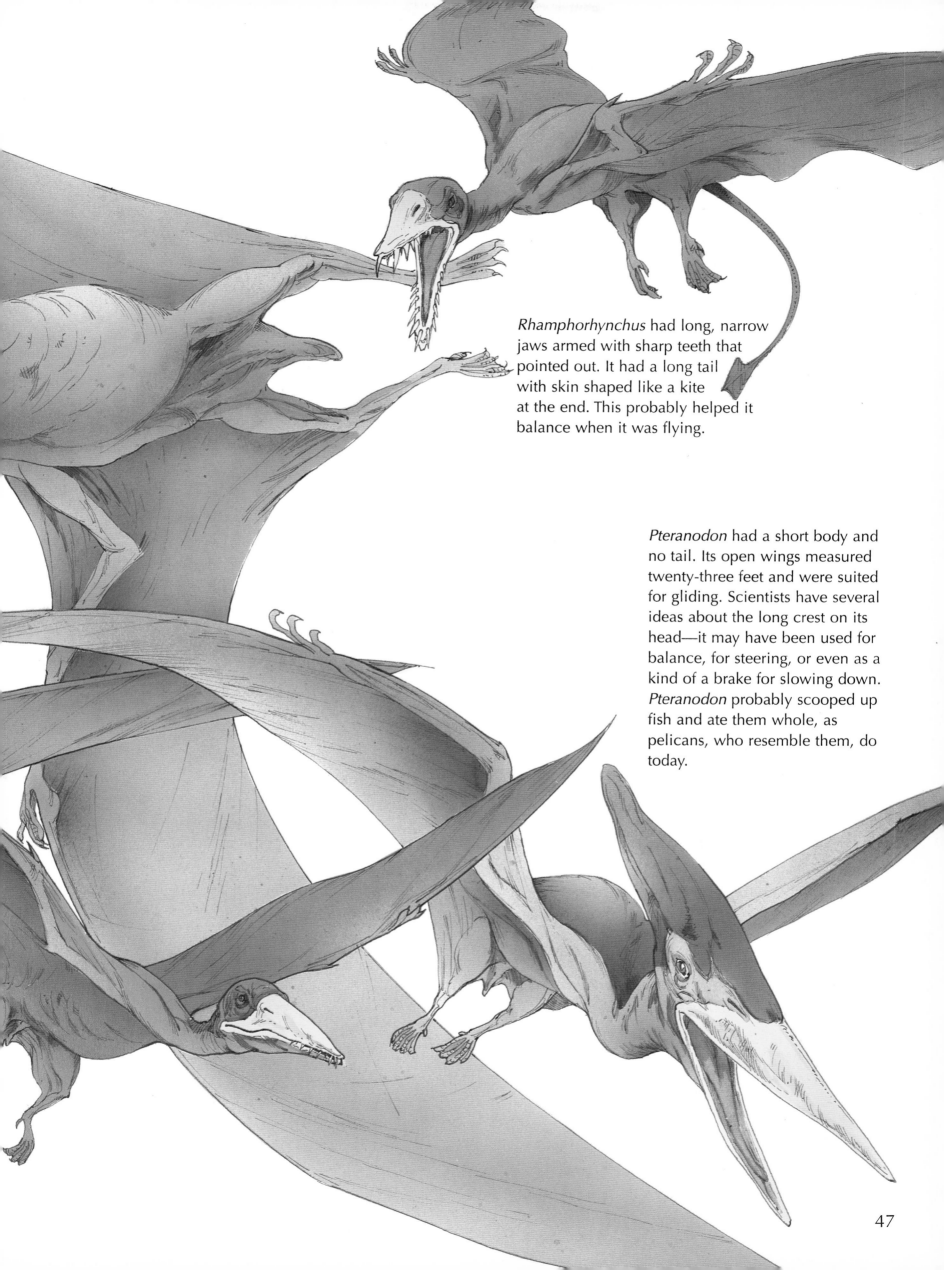

*Rhamphorhynchus* had long, narrow jaws armed with sharp teeth that pointed out. It had a long tail with skin shaped like a kite at the end. This probably helped it balance when it was flying.

*Pteranodon* had a short body and no tail. Its open wings measured twenty-three feet and were suited for gliding. Scientists have several ideas about the long crest on its head—it may have been used for balance, for steering, or even as a kind of a brake for slowing down. *Pteranodon* probably scooped up fish and ate them whole, as pelicans, who resemble them, do today.

# Marine reptiles

During the Age of Dinosaurs, when the dinosaurs were masters of the earth, other reptiles ruled the oceans of the world for more than 100 million years. One group of ocean reptiles, the Ichthyosaurs ("fish lizards"), resembled dolphins. They had long, smooth bodies like fish, but they breathed air. They did not lay eggs like other reptiles. Instead they gave birth to fully developed babies in the water.

Another group, the Plesiosaurs, did not look at all like fish. These enormous marine reptiles had long, unusual necks. They lived in the water, but came out onto dry land to lay their eggs.

The Mosasaurs were huge and terrifying sea creatures that looked like monstrous crocodiles.

*Kronosaurus* was a fierce hunter. Its jaws and teeth were larger and more powerful than the jaws of a *Tyrannosaurus rex!*

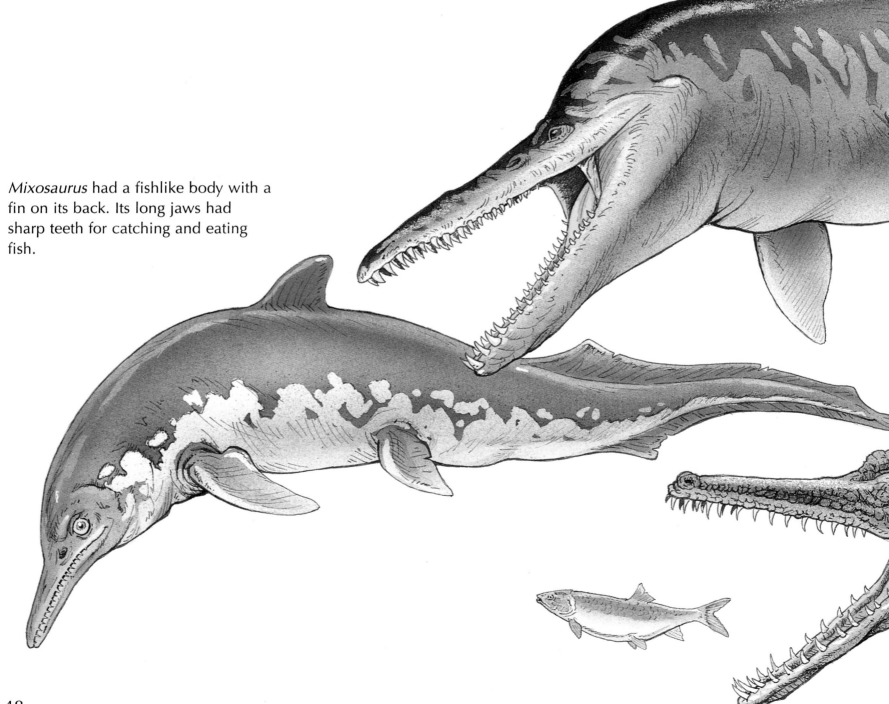

*Mixosaurus* had a fishlike body with a fin on its back. Its long jaws had sharp teeth for catching and eating fish.

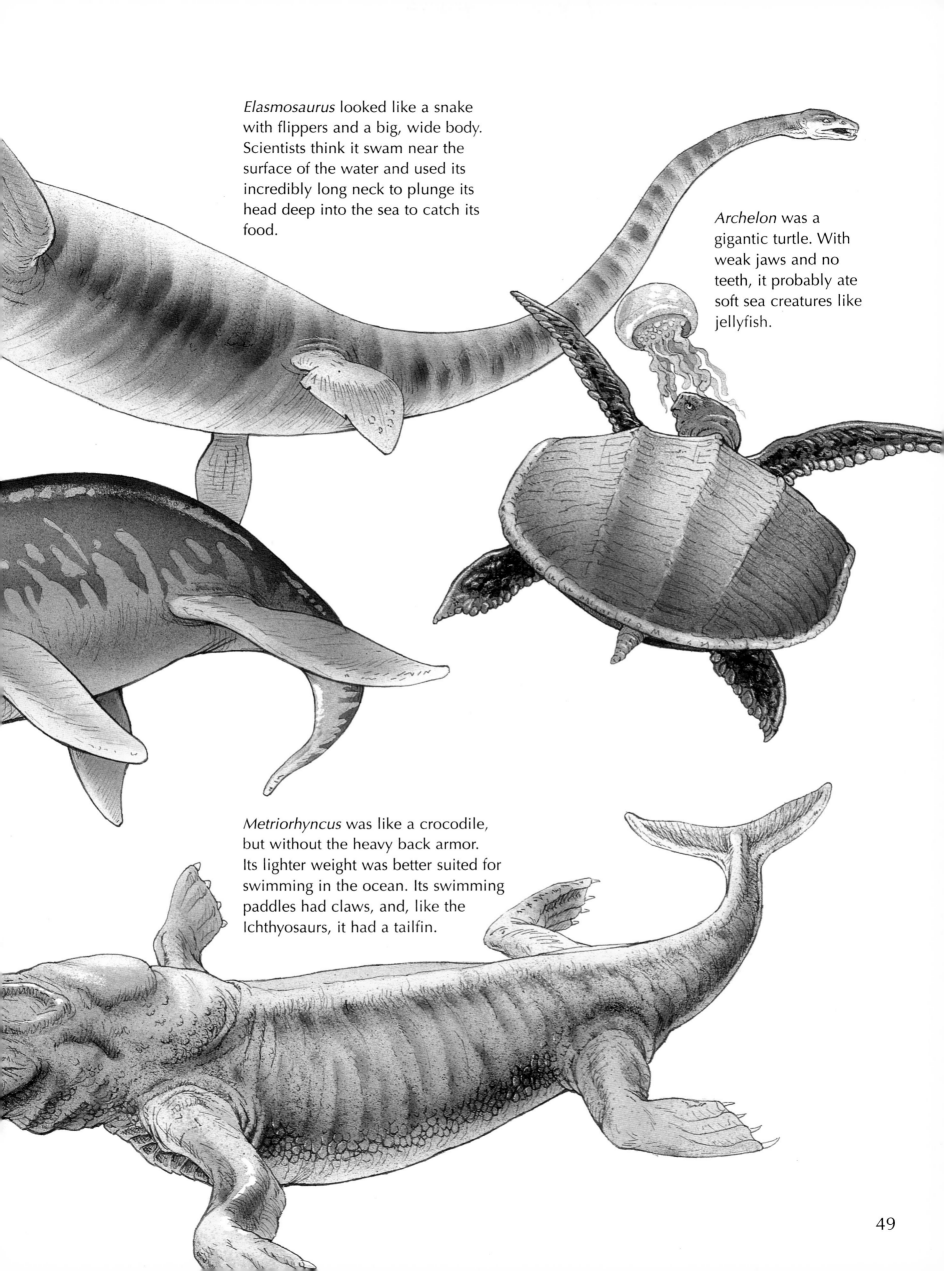

*Elasmosaurus* looked like a snake with flippers and a big, wide body. Scientists think it swam near the surface of the water and used its incredibly long neck to plunge its head deep into the sea to catch its food.

*Archelon* was a gigantic turtle. With weak jaws and no teeth, it probably ate soft sea creatures like jellyfish.

*Metriorhyncus* was like a crocodile, but without the heavy back armor. Its lighter weight was better suited for swimming in the ocean. Its swimming paddles had claws, and, like the Ichthyosaurs, it had a tailfin.

# Social life

Scientists have discovered fossils of dinosaur nests and groups of fossilized footprints. These give us important clues about the social life of dinosaurs.

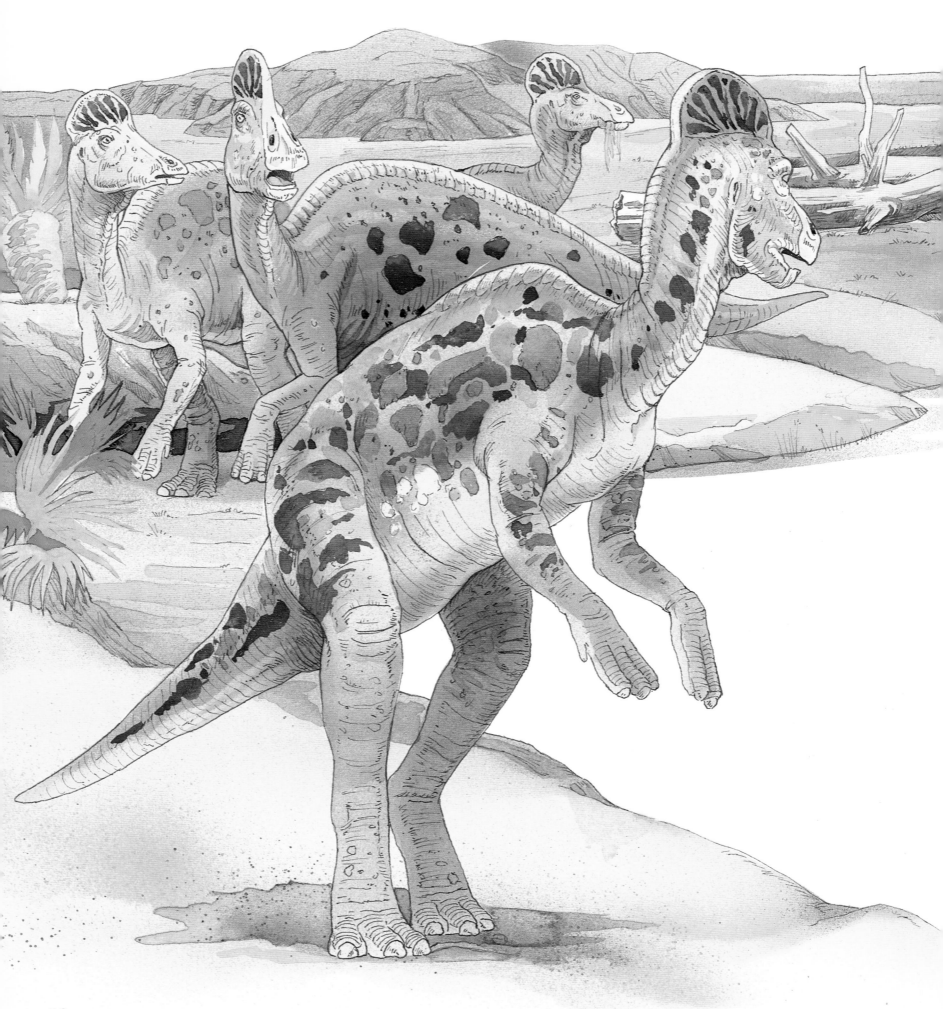

Plant-eaters, like Diplodocids and Ceratopsids, stayed together in large herds. They protected their young by keeping them in the middle of groups of grown-up dinosaurs. Living in groups of hundreds of dinosaurs could cause problems—more hungry mouths to feed, sicknesses spreading from one animal to another in the herd, more rivalry in selecting a mate. Still, dinosaurs were safer living in herds because they could join together to fight off their enemies. Even so, some meat-eaters, like *Deinonychus* and *Coelophysis,* were successful in attacking herds of larger dinosaurs because they hunted in packs and sneaked up on their prey. Animals in a herd probably "talked" to one another in some way, as scientists think the Hadrosaurs did with their crests.

Some dinosaurs made their nests very close to one another, and each mother dinosaur laid several eggs. The neighborhood mothers could help each other gather food and protect the eggs and baby dinosaurs.

# The end of the dinosaurs

Dinosaurs first appeared on earth about 225 million years ago. They ruled the world for 160 million years. Then, about 65 million years ago, the dinosaurs all disappeared, leaving behind only some fossils of their bones, teeth, footprints, armor plating, and eggs.

Scientists will never know why all the dinosaurs suddenly vanished, but they have a few different ideas to explain this mystery. Some scientists think that an asteroid or a gigantic meteorite crashed into the earth and made huge clouds of dust. These clouds blocked out all the light of the sun for many months or years. Without light, the plants would have all died. Without plants to eat, the herbivores that ate them would have died. And without these other dinosaurs to eat, the meat-eaters would have all died.

Scientists have other ideas, too:

Perhaps a big change in the weather over five or six million years caused most of the plants to die. Without food, the plant-eaters and then the meat-eaters would have all starved to death.

Maybe many small mammals evolved that liked to eat dinosaur eggs. If most of the dinosaur eggs were eaten, not enough young dinosaurs would have been born to take the place of the grown-ups as they grew old and died off.

A star might have exploded and showered radiation down upon the earth. Radiation sickness could have killed the dinosaurs. Or did some other virus or disease kill all the dinosaurs? The end of the dinosaurs is one of the biggest mysteries of all.

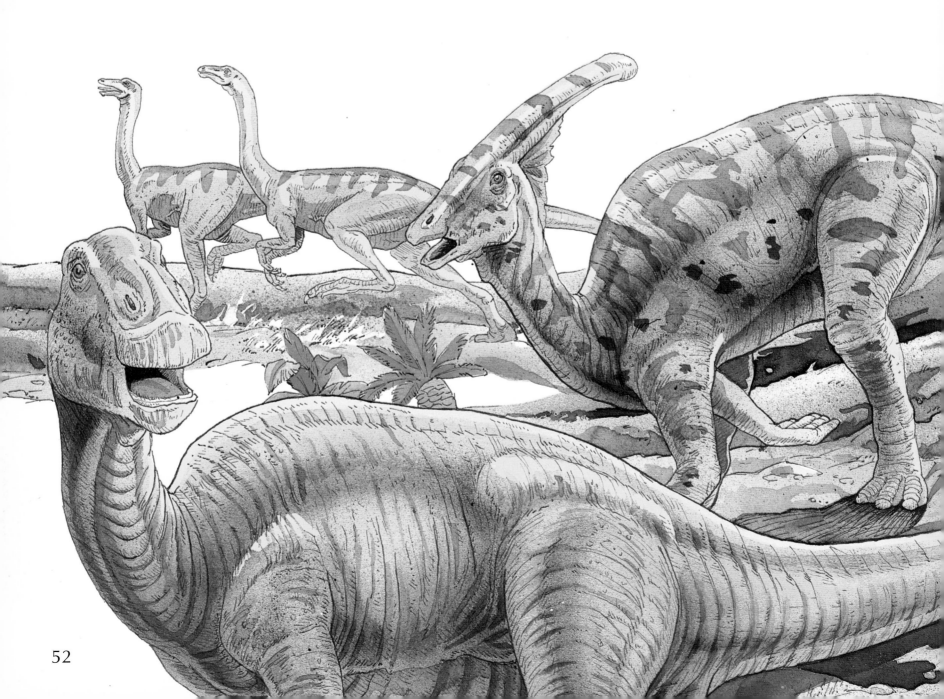

# Dinosaurs in the movies

It is fun to imagine what dinosaurs were like. Writers and movie makers think so, too, and have made dinosaurs the stars of many books and movies. We can enjoy the thrills and chills of these stories because we know we will never meet a real dinosaur. In some movies, made many years ago, the dinosaurs looked fake, like slow-moving robots. It was fairly easy to see that they were not really alive. But today, movie makers have learned many new special effects, and they can make dinosaurs look very real indeed!

In *Jurassic Park,* a film made by Steven Spielberg, the dinosaur robots really do look alive. *Jurassic Park* was first a book written by Michael Crichton. In this scary, made-up story, modern scientists figure out how to make real live dinosaurs. Spielberg's skilled artists and technicians built full-size models of some of the most famous dinosaurs, including fierce *Tyrannosaurus,* vicious *Velociraptor,* and gentle *Brachiosaurus.* They used special computers to make these lifelike robots move and act like real animals. The effect is terrifying.

# Myths and legends

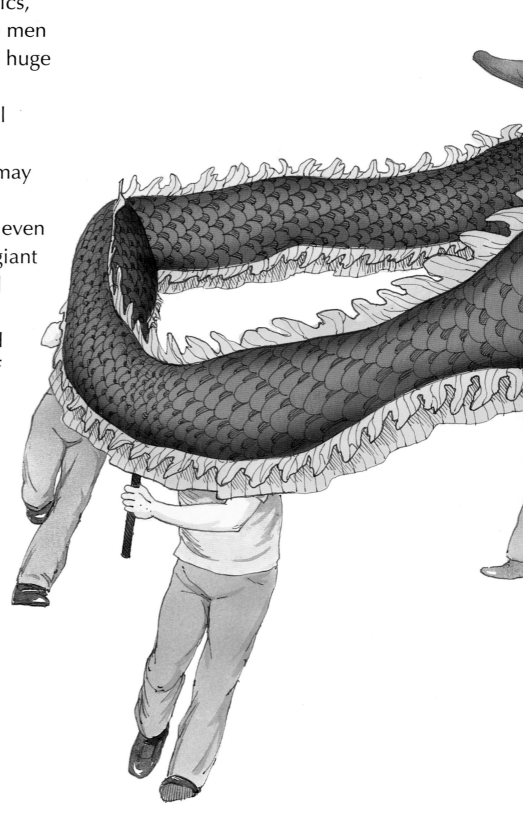

When talking about dinosaurs, it is easy to let your imagination run wild. You may shiver with fear and think of enormous, mean-tempered beasts. You may picture yourself face to face with one of these tremendous creatures. But remember, not one single human being has ever met a dinosaur on this earth. Dinosaurs were extinct for millions of years before the earliest human ancestors were born. Even so, many movies, comics, and cartoons still show prehistoric cave men armed with stone-tipped spears fighting huge dinosaurs—and actually winning!

As we have seen in this book, not all dinosaurs were enormous and vicious creatures. Some were fierce and some may have been quite gentle. Most were tremendous, but others were small and even graceful. Stories of dragons and other giant creatures appear in fables, legends, and myths from all over the world. Generations of storytellers have terrified and excited us with tales of monsters of the land, sea, and air. The earth was indeed home to mysterious giants, though not the monsters of these legends and stories. The awesome world of dinosaurs did exist long ago. But the best place to look for dinosaurs today is in a museum.

Look closely at this drawing of Saint George slaying a dragon. Doesn't the dragon look a bit like *Tyrannosaurus* with the wings of a Pterodactyl?

The dragon is an important part of Oriental folklore and beliefs. For the Chinese, the dragon is a symbol of good fortune. In this special parade to honor the dragon, a colorful paper dragon is carried through the streets.

57

# Showcase of dinosaurs

Which is your favorite dinosaur? Do you know that scientists have discovered more than 370 different kinds of dinosaurs so far, and there are probably many others. Here are eight of the most well-known ones.

**Apatosaurus**
Some scientists used to call this dinosaur *Brontosaurus.* It was a giant plant-eater with a heavy body and a long neck and tail.

**Triceratops**
This dinosaur was as heavy as an elephant. Its rhinoceros-like body and horned head may have protected it from its enemies.

**Tyrannosaurus**
Perhaps the most famous dinosaur of all, *Tyrannosaurus* was one of the largest and most powerful meat-eaters that ever lived.

**Deinonychus**
When *Deinonychus* stood up, it was shorter than a grown man. This vicious creature used its large curved claw for slashing its prey.

**Stegosaurus**
It's easy to recognize *Stegosaurus* with the triangular plates arranged along its back.

**Velociraptor**
One of the smaller, faster, smarter dinosaurs, *Velociraptor* was a meat-eater.

**Baryonyx**
This unusual dinosaur had a head like a crocodile and is the only dinosaur that is known to have eaten fish.

**Parasaurolophus**
Perhaps the long crest on the head of this "duck-billed" Hadrosaur was used for making sounds.

# Index